Life Beyond Your Parents' Mistakes

....

The Transforming Power
of God's Love

David Powlison

www.newgrowthpress.com

All Scripture quotations, unless otherwise indicated, are taken from the *Holy Bible*, New International Version®, NIV®. Copyright © 1973, 1978, 1984 by International Bible Society. Used by permission of Zondervan. All rights reserved.

New Growth Press, Greensboro, NC 27404
Copyright © 2010 by David Powlison.
All rights reserved. Published 2010.

Typesetting: Robin Black, www.blackbirdcreative.biz

ISBN-10: 1-935273-18-3
ISBN-13: 978-1-935273-18-9

Library of Congress Cataloging-in-Publication Data

Powlison, David, 1949-
   Life beyond your parents' mistakes : the transforming power of God's love / David Powlison.
     p. cm.
   Includes bibliographical references and index.
   ISBN-13: 978-1-935273-18-9 (alk. paper)
   ISBN-10: 1-935273-18-3 (alk. paper)
1. Adult children of dysfunctional families--Religious life.
2. Adult children of dysfunctional families--Psychology. 3. Christian life. I. Title.
   BV4596.A274P69 2010
   248.8'6--dc22

                                    2010003487

Printed in Canada

19 18 17 16 15 14 13 12   3 4 5 6 7

Sally grew up in a dangerous household. During her teen years, her father sexually molested her, putting a bitter icing on their miserable relationship. Though she became a Christian in high school, Sally felt that she could never know God as her Father. Her relationship with her earthly father was just too damaging. Now twenty-eight years old, she still tends to see God as untrustworthy, demanding, merciless, and unpredictable.

Keasha's mom was verbally abusive. She constantly criticized Keasha, nitpicking the smallest flaws. Anger and avoidance were the family's "standard operating procedure." Keasha has her own family now, but she still struggles to understand God's love for her. "How can I?" she said to me, "My mom made me feel worthless and unlovable. God's love can seem like just words to me."

Bill's father abandoned the family when Bill was three. Bill's mother worked two jobs to keep her family going. Bill never saw his dad again, and his mom was often preoccupied with the stress of being the sole caregiver for her family. Now thirty-six, Bill recently sought counseling because of his long-standing sense that "God is remote, like my parents were."*

Can You Know God's Love Even Though Your Own Parents Failed?

What about you? Perhaps you too feel like your parents' failures have kept you from knowing God's love and learning to love others. It is a common problem. And it does not have a snap-your-fingers solution. But it does have a true solution that patiently works in you. Take heart: God wants you to know and experience his love for you. He takes the time to make it more than mere words. His Word is full of reminders that he personally and powerfully loves his children:

> This is love: not that we loved God, but that he loved us and sent his Son as an atoning sacrifice for our sins. (1 John 4:10)
>
> If God is for us, who can be against us? He who did not spare his own Son, but gave him up for us

all—how will he not also, along with him, graciously give us all things? (Romans 8:31–32)

God has poured out his love into our hearts by the Holy Spirit, whom he has given us. (Romans 5:5)

You received the Spirit of sonship. And by him we cry, "Abba! Father." The Spirit himself testifies with our spirit that we are God's children. (Romans 8:15–16)

These aren't just words. God does what he says. They aren't just good intentions. He initiates a living relationship. These passages speak of two central ways that God shows his love to us. First, the historical fact: Jesus Christ went to an agonizing death out of love for his children. Second, the powerful dynamic within our hearts: the Holy Spirit pours out God's love in us to create the child's trusting response. *Did* God act in love in history? *Does* God act now in love within our hearts? Yes! God's love is effective, both then and now.

But what about when we feel disconnected from the historical fact of Christ's death for us and from the dynamic work of the Holy Spirit? What about Sally,

Keasha, and Bill? What about you? What do you do when you don't understand God's love for you? When the cross of Christ leaves you cold? When the Holy Spirit seems to be only a theory—not a daily help in times of trouble? What do you do when there is little or no "Abba, Father" in your heart?

People who struggle with understanding God's love for them often hear two thoughts from Christian counselors and others trying to help them.

- *Statement #1* is "You can't really appreciate God as Father if you had a poor relationship with your human parents."
- *Statement #2* is about counseling methods and often follows the first statement. It says, "If you have had parent problems in your personal history, you now need some sort of re-parenting or corrective emotional experience. You need the love of a parent substitute, therapist, mentor, or support group before you can experience God as a loving Father."

Are these statements true? If your parents were abusive, critical, neglectful or selfish, are you prevented from knowing God as a loving parent? Must you first experience a corrective human relationship to make "God is my Father" a nourishing reality?

When you carefully examine these statements, they turn out to be false. They distort the nature of the human heart, and they distort the reasons why people believe lies about God. Even worse, these statements deny the power and truth of how God actually works through his Word and Spirit. They replace Almighty God with an almighty psychotherapist, whose tolerance and affirmations prepare the heart for a god who will merely tolerate and affirm.

This is not to say that people with poor human parents don't often project those images onto the true God. They often do, and it's no wonder they go on to say that such a god is untrustworthy and unloving! Statement #1 reflects a common phenomenon: "I had a rotten parent, and I think God is rotten." But is the causal connection between these facts the real connection? Do people twist their view of God because they had sinful parents, or for some other reason? You must dig below the surface for the answer. Are there any people with bad parents who have a great relationship with God? Are there any people with good parents who have a rotten view of God?

For example, my former pastor lost his father in an accident when he was two. His mother soon remarried, and his stepfather was very abusive to him. But his stepfather's treatment of him did not keep him from understanding the love of God. Instead, the love of his heavenly Father became the most important thing in his life. He often said that growing up without a father's love made God's love all the more real to him. His favorite verse was 1 John 4:16: "And so we know and rely on the love God has for us."

Statement #2 also reflects a common experience: "It really made a difference to meet a person I could trust, and my relationship with God grew." Without a doubt, good, caring, and wise friends are a tremendous help in the change process. A godly counselor is like a godly parent in many ways. But is this explanation of change, however plausible, the right one? Again, you must dig. Do affirming human relationships correct the problem of a distorted view of God, or is there a different primary solution? Are there any people who know a person they trust, yet still think God is untrustworthy? Can a relationship with a person you trust mislead you further about God?

God Is My King, Shepherd, Master, Savior, and God

Our response to these two statements should start by noting that sinful human parents are not unique in misrepresenting God. *All* of the words God uses to describe himself have disappointing human parallels. Consider these examples:

God is King. Human rulers are frequently weak, distant, cruel, or corrupt. Who is in your mind when you think about what God the King is like? Rulers who accurately reflect God have always been rare. Yet your experience—however bad—needn't prevent you from knowing God as a just King and a merciful Judge. God himself tells you about good, bad, and mediocre kings so you can learn to tell the difference. The Bible also shows and tells what sort of king God is. The question is, which do you allow to dictate your perception of God: the Word or personal experience? If you look at God only through the lens of your human experience, you misunderstand him. But when you listen, the Holy Spirit speaks through the Word to reinterpret your life experiences. This truth then goes on to shape your perceptions of future experience.

The LORD is my shepherd. When it comes to human shepherds, few are like Philip Keller's winsome portrayal of the care and wisdom of the shepherd's craft (*A Shepherd Looks at Psalm 23*). What if any real-life shepherds you knew were ignorant laborers or drunken drifters? Or what if all you've known are storybook scenes of lambs and fair youths gamboling in green meadows? Is either picture helpful in understanding God? Does that mean that Psalm 23 is powerless to strengthen you until you know a Philip Keller-type shepherd? Of course not.

Think also about the shepherds of God's flock you've known. Some people can point with joy to a "godly pastor who made such an impact on my life." But other people grew up under false teachers—greedy, willful, and arrogant men like those in Ezekiel 34. Does this mean that you can't be comforted that the Lord is a shepherd until you know a godly pastor? Ezekiel 34 and John 10 argue the opposite. God assumes we can hear comfort straight from him even if people have betrayed our trust: "I am against these evil shepherds, and I, the good shepherd, will myself come and take care of you, my flock." The existence of perversity does not make us blind to purity. Get first things first. The Holy Spirit often *uses* godly shepherds but he does not *require* them. He is powerful enough to reveal the Chief Shepherd even without noble human models.

The Lord is my master, and I am his bond servant. How do people typically experience authority figures—bosses, commanding officers, CEOs, management? Often there is rivalry, estrangement, manipulation, and suspicion between masters and underlings. Literal slavery has always been full of degradation and resentment. Yet God chose a word that is loaded with negative experience and expects us to experience it as a delight. He portrays himself as a kind Master and us as willing slaves. What a shock Paul's language must have been to resentful or despairing servants—but how liberating, once they grasped the point! Again, God uses one-sided experience to point to two-sided truth. There are both good and bad master-servant relationships. Will you believe God or the world you've known? The Holy Spirit is able to renew our minds to trust the Lord.

God is my Savior, Rescuer, and Helper. We often have good reason to flee human beings who like to play the savior by rescuing or fixing others. They have a "messiah-complex" and are proud, meddlesome, self-righteous, and controlling. It's no fun being "helped" by such a helper! If you have known only pseudo-saviors, are you prevented from knowing Jesus Christ as your Savior? Amazingly, somehow God seems to be able to reveal himself as utterly Godly without utterly godly people showing the way.

The LORD is God. This is the ultimate example. What is the typical human experience of "God"? Depending on who you listen to, God is a philosophical abstraction, your higher power, an idol, an experiential high during meditation, a remote tyrant, a good buddy, creative energy, a benign grandfather, or even yourself. All these images grossly misshape God. Does that mean it is impossible to know the living and true God if I have spent my life believing such false images? The Bible everywhere rejects such an idea and offers instead to "open their eyes and turn them from darkness to light" (Acts 26:18). God is in the business of changing people's minds; he is not hindered by distortions. He can reveal himself, "[shining] in our hearts to give us the light of the knowledge of the glory of God in the face of Christ" (2 Corinthians 4:6). Life experience is not supreme; neither are the lies that people believe. God is, and he alone trumps what we bring to the table.

In each of these examples, it does not make sense to say that life experience dictates a person's reality. On the contrary, the very experience of disappointing and distorted images can make you long to know the real King, Shepherd, Master, Savior, and God! You might say, "My pastor never taught me about God. How I rejoice that

Hebrews 13:20–21 is true, that the great Shepherd of the sheep shed his blood for me and teaches me to do his will." "My boss is manipulative and deceptive. How I rejoice that Ephesians 6:5–8 is becoming true in me and I can serve Christ with integrity instead of being bitter or fearful!" "The God I grew up hearing about seemed like a remote killjoy. Praise the real God that Psalm 36 is true, and he is an immediate refuge and a fountain of love, light, and joy!"

Clearly, our fallen experience need not control us. Yet for many, the truth that "God is Father" seems to be the exception. They *do* feel that their knowledge of God the Father is controlled by the earthly parallel. So we turn to the second question: Must your own father dictate the meaning of that phrase until a substitute human father puts a new spin on it?

But Is God My Father?

Concepts from our psychologized culture saturate the way people (even Christian people) think about themselves and others. The source for the idea that your parents determine your view of the heavenly Father is psychodynamic psychology, not the Bible. Men such as Sigmund Freud and Erik Erikson rightly observed that people often create their own gods. Their psychodynamic theory made this "from the bottom up" pattern *the* explanation for our ideas of God. It denied that the real God reveals himself "from the top down." The psychodynamic god was a projection of the human psyche. Popular versions of this idea now permeate our culture.

"If my father didn't love me, I can't know God as a loving Father." This idea rings a bell in the human heart. But when we remember that our hearts are naturally distorted, we start to see different reasons why this explanation sounds so convincing to us. All sinners manufacture false images of God, and human fathers are prime models from which to work. As sinners, we duck responsibility for our unbelief, blaming others and savoring the role of victim. When we project lies and faulty images onto God, we may prefer to point to parents as the cause rather than looking to the activities of our own hearts. The psychological "insight" caters to our sinful human tendency to find excuses and reasons for unbelief.

In an earlier generation, a common excuse for unbelief was, "The church is full of hypocrites, so I don't want anything to do with God." That was more willful and bitter: "Get lost, God." Today, the tone is more self-pitying: "I just can't seem to trust God." But the net effect is the same. No cry of "Abba, Father" springs from the heart. "My father didn't love me, so my self-centeredness, self-pity, and unbelief have an underlying reason. Somebody else caused my problems; somebody else must fix them."

The therapeutic technique follows logically from these assumptions. "Your parents were distant and mean. You think of God as distant and mean. I, your therapist, am interested in you and kind. Knowing my love will let you think of God as like me, interested in you and kind." When stated so bluntly, that's a shocking statement. That's why it's usually insinuated, so it sneaks up on people.

The point here is important: Such "re-parenting" not only ignores God's living Word and the life-giving

Spirit; it also replaces one false image of God with another. The dissatisfying god manufactured by the human soul, supposedly because of bad parents, can now be remanufactured in the image of a satisfying therapist.

It's easy to see that the living and true God is not like an abusive, rejecting, capricious parent. The real God sent Jesus Christ on a mission of love to save unacceptable people. But God is not like the benign, all-accepting therapist either. The real God has just anger and an unchanging standard, and those he loves are "helpless, ungodly, sinners, enemies" (Romans 5). He is merciful, not all-accepting. The real God is not a devil, but neither is he Carl Rogers or Mr. Rogers. The "re-parenting" approach has a faulty view of who the Father is and what a parent ought to be. It knows that cruelty and neglect are wrong, but it replaces such sins with supreme confidence in the therapist's powers and affirmations of the self. There is no authoritative truth, no dying to self, and no crucified Savior in this version of love. Am I saying that caring counselors and friends are irrelevant to change? Of course not! One needn't choose between truth and love: people grow in the way Ephesians 4:15–16 describes. My point is simply that we need to get first things first so that our vision of human love connects with God's love, rather than competes with it.

People change when the Holy Spirit brings the love of God to their hearts through the gospel. Whoever receives the Spirit of adoption as God's child learns to cry out, "Abba, Father." People change when they see that they are responsible for what they believe about God. Life experience is no excuse for believing lies; the world and the devil don't excuse the flesh. People change when truth becomes clearer and brighter than previous life experience. We change when our ears hear and our eyes see what God tells us about himself:

> For the LORD comforts his people
> and will have compassion on his afflicted ones.
> But Zion said, "The LORD has forsaken me,
> the Lord has forgotten me."
> "Can a mother forget the baby at her breast

and have no compassion on the child she has borne?
Though she may forget, I will not forget you!
See, I have engraved you on the palms of my
hands." (Isaiah 49:13–16)

He does not treat us as our sins deserve
> or repay us according to our iniquities.
For as high as the heavens are above the earth,
> so great is his love for those who fear him;
as far as the east is from the west,
> so far has he removed our transgressions from us.
As a father has compassion on his children,
> so the LORD has compassion on those who fear
him. (Psalm 103:10–13)

These things are true: both the promise of compassion and the actions that express compassion. Through them, God comforts the fears of both the sufferers and sinners.

Do people come to know *this* God because human counselors skillfully re-parent them? No, and the very attempt to make that a counseling paradigm is idolatrous. But aren't good counselors like good fathers and mothers? Yes. As the apostle Paul says:

> But we were gentle among you, like a mother caring for her little children. We loved you so much that we were delighted to share with you not only the gospel of God but our lives as well, because you had become so dear to us. Surely you remember, brothers, our toil and hardship; we worked night and day in order not to be a burden to anyone while we preached the gospel of God to you. You are witnesses, and so is God, of how holy, righteous and blameless we were among you who believed. For you know that we dealt with each of you as a father deals with his own children, encouraging, comforting, and urging you to live lives worthy of God, who calls you into his kingdom and glory. (1 Thessalonians 2:7–12)

Why should a counselor be like this? Because God is like this. The difference between Paul's pattern and re-parenting therapy lies on the surface. Did Paul "re-parent" the Thessalonians so that, now knowing and changed by Paul's love, they would be able to envision God as loving? No, that's exactly backwards and even blasphemous.

Paul was gentle, vigorous, caring, and authoritative as a parent-counselor carrying the Father's message. The love of the Father changes people, and it changed Paul. Knowing divine love, he could embody love—a love that was the fruit and the vehicle of the message he pressed on his hearers. God is primary. The human agent is significant but secondary, dependent on the One who is primary.

The modern re-parent/therapist reverses this. The human counselor is primary. God is either irrelevant or secondary. The issue at stake is not whether or not counselors should be patient, kind, and generous. First Corinthians 13 settles that. But in God's drama of redemption, who will play the lead, and who will be the supporting actor?

If your father didn't love you, you can know the love of the Father. A godly counselor (or parent or friend) will often be instrumental. But the key to change lies between you and God, not between you and that other person.

Practical Strategies for Change

Let's look at how these truths helped Sally, Bill, and Keasha. As Sally acknowledged, "For years I thought I could never know God as my Father because I had such a rotten relationship with my dad. But then I came to realize that my biggest problem was *me*, not God *or* my father. My belief system was all messed up. I was projecting lies onto God and not believing what was true about him!"

Sally began to feed her faith with the truth that God the Father *is* faithful, merciful, and consistent. He patiently worked with her, disciplining her and teaching her to know the merciful, generous truth about him. Sally saw that her view of God was not *caused* by her life experience but by what her own heart had done with her experience of being wronged. As Sally turned to God, her mind was renewed, and she was progressively freed to let go of old disappointments, bitterness, fears, and demands. She became able to say wholeheartedly, "Give thanks to the LORD, for he is good, for his steadfast love endures forever."

Keasha spent time pondering 1 John 4 and Romans 5. She asked the Spirit to pour God's love into her. She asked other Christians to pray for her that she would know and understand God's love for her. The more she thought about Jesus' death on the cross and how his heavenly Father sent his own Son to lay down his life for her, the more she was struck by the contrast between God's love for her and her mother's nitpicking. She said, "I saw the difference between my mom's very imperfect love and God's perfect love for me, and I was filled with thankfulness for the love of my heavenly Father." She took God to heart.

Her growing sense of God's care for her, despite her difficult childhood, gave her the ability to forgive her mom for how she had treated her. She said, "I realized that my mom was wrong, but some of the ways I responded to her were wrong as well. Now I am learning, one small step at a time, how to return good for evil as Jesus did."

As Bill wrestled with his sense that "God is remote, like my father was," there were three significant components to change. First, he realized that he, like all of us, tended to view his life experience as a technicolor blockbuster film, while the Bible seemed a dull, black-and-white silent movie. The flesh produces this state of affairs by interpreting life through the lens of its lies and desires. Bill began with two key truths about God as Father. First, God *is* abounding in mercy (Psalm 103; 2 Corinthians 1:2–5). Second, God *is* committed to meet his children directly, to teach, to bless, and to transform (John 15:2; Hebrews 12:1–14). Bill prayed and meditated these truths into his life. As he learned to repent of the lies he had believed, he found the Father becoming vivid.

Second, in the process, Bill faced sins he had been avoiding. The flesh is deceitful. He found that his sentence, "God is remote, like my father was," came in part from buying into pop psychology's convenient and self-excusing diagnosis. It's true, God *did* seem distant. And Bill's father *had* been absent. But on examination the two things proved to be minimally related, much like saying, "I'm angry because I'm an Aries." Early in Bill's Christian life, God had not seemed remote at all. But some very specific patterns of sin—sexual fantasy, manipulating and avoiding people, laziness, love of money—lay beneath Bill's recurrent sense of God's distance. Psychology had turned his childhood relationship with parents into a magic wand to explain everything that was wrong in his present life. The Bible offered Bill a more concrete and life-transforming explanation.

Third, Bill found some good friends and models (Proverbs 13:20; 1 Thessalonians 2:7–13). He had been quite isolated. He found people to know and be known by, to love and be loved by. These people did not substitute for God and re-parent Bill. They were fellow children of the Father, seeking to grow up into the Father's image. Through it all Bill began to read God into his experience—to trust and obey God—rather than continuing to read God through his life experience. No surprise, his relationship with God was increasingly transformed objectively and experientially.

Can you know God as Father even if your human parents were violent, deceptive, cold, critical...or even just occasionally disappointing? The Bible says, YES! Listen and believe, and join in fellowship with other children of the Father.

How to Grow in Knowing God's Love

Here is a simple summary of the way to grow in the knowledge of God your Father, even if your parents failed you (and of course all parents *have* sinned against their children).

1. Identify and take responsibility for the specific lies, false beliefs, desires, expectations, and fears that dim your relationship with God.

2. Find specific truths in the Bible that contend with those lies and cravings. There ought to be a battle going on within you daily as God's light and love

battle your darkness.

3. Turn to God for mercy and help, asking the Spirit of truth to renew you, to pour out his love freely.

4. Take responsibility for the particular sins you express toward your parents and, as generalized patterns, toward other people: bitterness, willfulness, avoidance, blame-shifting, brooding, fears, people-pleasing, slander, lying, self-pity, etc.

5. Turn to God for mercy and help. Ask for the Spirit of love to enable you to bear his fruit thankfully.

6. Identify the specific sins committed against you. Parents who are selfish or hostile, who lie or betray trust, who duck responsibility, are parents who do evil. The love of God gives you courage to look evil in the eye. Identifying wrong helps you know what to forgive. It also makes clear what God calls you to tackle constructively. You

need humility to recognize that some wrongs may only be perceived wrongs—products of your own expectations—not real wrongs. Repenting of your own sins clears your mind to sort out evil done from evil merely perceived. You also need a renewed mind to understand that some things you were told or you assumed were right may actually be wrong.

7. Ponder the good things your parents did for you. Often bitterness and disappointment cloud the love that was shown. There are some parents who seem to incarnate evil, but most are a mix of love and selfishness.

8. The Father gives us power to return good for evil rather than evil for evil. He remakes his children like his Son, Jesus. Come up with a plan for specific changes in how you deal with your parents and their wrongs: forgiving, giving love, seeking forgiveness, forbearing, confronting constructively,

refocusing your attention, pouring your energies into God's calling, etc.

9. Find wise friends to pray for you, hold you accountable, encourage, and counsel you. Faith in God our Father is catching. Wisdom for living as a peacemaker and a son of God is also catching. "The companion of the wise becomes wise."

The Father is seeking worshipers and creating children who know him. So ask, seek, and knock, and come to know him as he is.

* All names are fictitious and personal details have been changed.

Simple, Quick, Biblical

Advice on Complicated Counseling Issues
for Pastors, Counselors, and Individuals

MINIBOOK
CATEGORIES

- Singles
- Marriage & Family
- Medical & Psychiatric Issues
- Personal Change

YOURSELF | GIVE TO A FRIEND | DISPLAY IN YOUR CHURCH OR MINISTRY

New Growth Press

Go to **www.newgrowthpress.com** or call **877.647.2233** to purchase individual minibooks or the entire collection. Durable acrylic display stands are also available to house the minibook collection.